BEYOND THIS INFERNO

DANTE' DURUISSEAU

To my father, thank you for your guidance

BEYOND THIS INFERNO

THE BEGINNING

The light became brighter and easier to see,

Blinded I was after being enveloped in the darkness for so long.

Stretching my hands forward, seeking guidance to my great exodus, the earth of my tomb seemed to show me the path.

At last, I found my way amongst people of the living who greeted me with joy and kindness. I asked, "How long have I slept?" "Three days dear Son of Man and we have patiently awaited your return."

My vision focused to a scene of horror, a world falling apart into the oblivion of chaos. Rivers were red with as blood, the sky dark from smoke and at times the earth shook with such violence I found myself falling to the ground.

The waters knew no peace, even the Sun had moved from its set course. No longer did it set in the West and rise in the East. Some of the people walked in what seemed a drunken and lost state, others panicked and ran to and from mad like one who has lost their mind.

So violent man had become, that he murdered without truly understanding why. The mothers abandoned their children, giving birth in the street then walking away from the life she just gave.

How did the world come to this? Perhaps I am dead, and this is the destination called hell or perhaps I am Christ resurrected sent to bring order to this chaos.

WE ARE ONE (INTRODUCTION)

Am I to paint a picture with words?

Volunteering your subconscious to be the canvas on which I imprint an image. Close your eyes or leave them open, my light will shine upon your mind and create the images I desire you to see. Our third eye is wide open, and we comprehend each other as we truly are. Metaphysically connected, you reading these words is how I am injected into your spiritual womb where I am a thought implanted, growing becoming one with you and you one with me. In time you will give birth to new concepts and ideas that are a mix of your and my subconscious, such a beautiful creation of thought it will be.

In this great river of energy our planets have orbited, and we are now aware of each other's existence, therefore WE ARE, and TO BE is a great explosion of chaos that brings about a new order of an ever-expanding universe. Frequencies connected, we are now pitched and in tune, each one of us a unique instrument in this Grand Chorus of sound vibrating through space and time.

I know you; you know me. We were both companions before being breathed into this human form and now here we are connected again. Read my words, absorb me. Every letter and syllable bringing us closer and closer.

We are now . . . ONE.

The Body

Ode to the human body, amazing you are, praise and thanks to The One who shaped you. Many of Hallowed Books say you were formed from the clay of the Earth, such a wonderful Potter who has fashioned us then gave us life. Do we appreciate this vehicle that transports our souls through this physical realm?

We marvel at the materials creations of man, but have we truly admired this ensemble of flesh and bone which we carry until we are free from it? What technology can truly compare to this bio-mechanical vessel. Enthralled we are with the forward movement of Artificial Intelligence, but have we forgotten this Natural Intelligence? Put together by One who has designed all (seen and unseen).

Through the ages we have learned much about the universe, yet within our own selves are galaxies unexplored. Look into the mirror and contemplate your being, genetic memory fashioned and formed into a physical entity, exploring the many phases of this current realm until death, and even after that is it truly over?

* * *

It seems we are an existence inside an existence, inside many more existences, worlds beyond our own understanding. Aware yet unaware of so much, yet a new awareness is awakened every day. New realities connect us to the networks of greatness that has always been aware of us.

Ode to the human experience!

FACE OF TRUTH

Sweet Savannah I want to see what you look like without the makeup on. Please understand, I don't mind prettification with a little eyeliner and lipstick, but true beauty without the mask turns me on. Let those eye lashes be real, no taste of powder on my lips when your face and neck I feel.

What's the true color of those eyes?

When I awaken to you in the morning I wish not to be surprised. What's hidden behind all that mess on your face? When I bite your neck sweet flesh is all I wish to taste. True splendor is maintained through self-care, if done properly the evidence shows from the bottom of your feet to every strand of your hair.

Do you consume the swine? It is said that you are what you eat. My tongue journeys between the legs of only Kosher meat. Please stay away from cigarettes and alcohol which makes you age before your time. Keep yourself educated, for there is nothing more amazing than a woman with a beautiful mind

Must you subject your body to plastic surgeries and alterations? Doesn't exercise and healthy eating keep everything in place? Sweet Savannah I want to see you without all that makeup on your face.

MERCY TO MAN

Dear Lord,

You are beyond Merciful and Compassionate. The sin of man is plenty, yet you grant him sustenance and provision. You made the earth livable for him, establishing the perfect balance above and below, yet he is still ungrateful. The sun is neither too far nor too close yet even on the hot days you grant him shade and water to satisfy his thirst. Oceans are held back from the land; food is provided to him from those salt and sweet waters that through Your Greatness you keep divided. Who does man think he is walking about as if he is a mighty god himself? Has he not recognized how insignificant he is in this ever-expanding sea of creation?

Once a sticky liquid then placed in a womb to grow, so powerless they are without their guardians to feed and protect them, yet they have the audacity to be arrogant and filled with pride. If the earth turned against him, if nature rebelled and the heavens fell upon them, their false pride would turn them to the sincerest of prayers. Forgive us Lord, I'm sure a day approaches when all must come to an end including Your Mercy towards man.

THE PEN

The pen has been abandoned, my hands lay idle with useless work, back hunched over with face lost in a screen of foolishness. Absorbed into the goings on of a cycle of work, mindlessness, and low-quality sleep. The mouse scurries about the labyrinth yet never finds the cheese, then he sleeps the days away to rest up for the chase tomorrow, but he will die in his never-ending pursuit.

This pen has been neglected, these hands have been busy with a perverted deed that drains a man of his strength and creative energy. Indulged in instant satisfaction and that chemical reaction in the brain that temporarily makes things better yet stunts growth and development. I have finally gotten over myself, now the pen is my friend again. My hands are no longer idle, I will continue this journey.

THE WESTERN WHITE MINDS

Let us explore the westernized white mind,

Take a journey into this place and see what we find. Some will say they do not see color,

Well dear sir/madam, are you color blind?

Respect for the tone God has given me you will have, at least, I hope.

Is pretending to not see color the way you cope, with histories past misdeeds?

What is it that you need?

The history of white supremacy was fueled by materialistic greed,

An indoctrination that has set, to complete the process of world domination,

You will say, "that was in the past," yet if I look back into my father's time,

I will find segregation.

History books in schools and movies never fail to remind us of cotton fields and slavery,

Yet for your stories, its explorations, heroes, patriots, and tales of bravery when dealing with those savages.

To me it is such a pity,

Because if you look at the true history of Europe/ Europeans, it is a story that is not so pretty.

Many deleted pages,

From your times being prisoners in the freezing lands all the way to the dark ages.

There was disorder and chaos in your own worlds,

Have you forgotten your disputes over religious and political beliefs?

Your inquisitions that tortured and killed Europeans should leave you silent when speaking of the religious division in the Middle East.

Shall I continue?

When you were not slaughtering each other, you ruthlessly divided the darker nations up devouring them finding little to no mercy within you.

Hiding behind Christ, you hid your evil intent behind cross and steel,

Claiming that you were doers of God's work and the savages of the world you came to heal.

Uncivilized you say,

Yet while you were crawling in the cold bitter dark, many worlds were already finding a way,

Stars mapped and new civilized nations growing every day.

Your brethren to the south were not the fathers of their knowledge.

Long before Socrates and Aristotle there were sacred schools of learning, ancient universities, and college.

No more than initiates into the sacred rites, The darker people were never savages,

It is these people who brought forth the light. But you will never give credit to where it is due,

It is your arrogant way of telling the world, "I am better than you."

I must admit that you have conquered, and you have conquered well, But your ways of rulership are leading the world straight to hell.

A world moved by materialism and greed, Is a world that cannot truly succeed.

You are not supreme because of the color of your skin,

You even painted Christ white, yet you have tainted the world with bloodshed and sin.

The westernized white mind is a mind that is lost,

and any who follow behind him and his ways will forever pay a horrible cost.

-Isms & -Ocracies

I'm not one to be caught up in the many -isms and -ocracies,
The poor proletariat and bourgeoisie hypocrisy.

Yes, we have the right to vote,

But sometimes it seems Democrat and Republican are two tyrants on the same boat.

When the vessel begins to sink, the wealthy amongst them will flee, Leaving the poor and middle class to die in the cold unyielding seas. Their oratory skills impress,

Yet the truth of their intentions they will never confess.

Boasting and bragging of their achievements though they have achieved nothing at all,

Yet they clear themselves of catastrophes sometimes before the wall even begins to fall.

Insider trading, confidential power broker meetings,

Arranged assassinations and staged coups long before the foreign president puts out his hand for greeting.

The eagle lands where it is not invited, Claiming to put out fires which it has ignited.

The iron fist covered in a velvet glove of a hidden totalitarian, the false face a of a caring democracy loving shepherd, but heart of a hateful Aryan.

The other isms are no better. Behind that red iron curtain, they will crush the citizens hopes with the hammer and ruthlessly reap their property with that sickle.

Much of man's ways are doomed to fail,

They promise the people heaven yet lead them straight to hell.

DAJJAL

A man stood looking far in the distance with a look of worry but also excitement. I asked him, "what are you staring at so nervously?" His response shocked me he when he said, "I am glancing towards Jerusalem waiting for Jesus to come back.

According to the signs,

it must be that time for him to return to slay the evil one and establish justice and peace in the land. The waters have risen, seas have turn to blood,

there is hatred in the land with not a single bit of love, even the earth begins to rebel, earthquakes and volcanoes make this place a living hell.

Disease and pestilence have riddled the earth,

a mother abandons her child soon as she gives birth, there is nowhere to run and hide,

the children are so stressed they are committing suicide.

Dark clouds of war have blocked the sun, Tyrannical governments rule by the barrel of a gun.

There is no peace,

it has been held hostage by an evil one-eyed beast who says
he is waiting for Jesus to come back also.
He calls himself Dajjal."

HUMANITY

What will come of humanity?

This is a question that weighs heavy on my sanity. We've been through much in this short period of time, Seeking that utopia to give us all a piece of mind.

Dreams have turned to nightmares from man-made -isms and -oracies, Especially for the poor who become victims of hypocrisy.

Promises made become unfulfilled,

The unfortunate pawns of society are sent to war to kill and be killed. What will we fight over next?

Battles fought over political opinion, religion, race and sex. Some how we find a dividing line,

These borders are invisible existing only in our minds. Acting as if we have some other place to go,

Cutting down our trees and polluting the places where our water resources flow,

Aren't we all sisters and brothers descended from one mother and father?

Originating from one place then spread far and wide,

From the many different islands to the countryside. Unique are our languages and colors,

Even our fingerprints are different from each other. The basics foundations of our existence are the same, The seed, the egg and from the womb we came.

We are the vicegerents of this Earth, yet power and dominance we have abused.

We have become lost in our own illusions,

Out of touch with reality, trapped in a labyrinth of confusion. Surely, we have gone astray,

As Dante' in the dark forest we lost our way.

Some suffer in silence,

While others act out with rage and violence. Have we become servants of our lower selves?

Compromising our mental, physical and spiritual health.

Unfortunate is the price paid for materialism and a false sense of beauty, And for this temporary pleasure we sacrifice all moral and divine duties. Short is this stay,

Much of which the masses spend on foolish distraction and play. Little is truly taken seriously,

Except by the genius mind who is moved by constant curiosity. He/she looks at the world desiring to know more.

Seeking knowledge, always standing at understanding and wisdom's door.

The foolish speak loudly of non-sense and violence,

While the Great Secrets are revealed to the wise ones who move in calculated silence.

He/she has gained mastery over his animalistic ways,

They are in control of their tongues and that which is between their legs. Elevated beyond the earthly realm and flesh,

Achieving true humanity with every breath.

We are human.

Dante Duruisseau

THE VIRUS

It came from China, Wuhan to be exact.

Probably has been hidden for some time, but there are claims it came from a bat. Some believe that it was man made. Perhaps a weapon for warfare meant to kill the biological way. Whatever the case it became a secret that finally leaked. The Chinese government silenced anyone who dared to speak. God bless the rebels who blew the whistle.

It was too late, a single sneeze or cough propelled it like a missile. No Chinese New Year just millions on lock down. A city usually busy became a silent ghost town. Governments thought quarantining whole metropolises would stop the spread, But the numbers continued to increase of the sick and dead.

The Chinese Government tried to sensor the internet and control what was said, The People desired freedom, yet they were silenced by an army of red.The virus was given the name Corona, and she moved like a deadly breeze, Finding its way onto to cruise ships and finally overseas.

Could this be part of some conspiracy or sadistic plan? Either way Corona ventured from mainland China, attacking

South Korea and Japan.

Many U.S. officials didn't take it seriously,

Governments continued to remain silent but that only caused many to react furiously. Before the virus, the People of Hong Kong was putting up a fight, striving against their government, for democracy and human rights.

Here was Corona wreaking havoc on the populations of Earth. Knocking on the door of the U.K. Even making threats to the American way. The virus continued to spread every day.

With only profit and pleasure in mind there was the breaking of quarantine by disease riddled cruise ships. Time had come for the whole world to be sick.

Corona was a ruthless magician and making humanity vanish was to be its greatest trick. Yet humanity by The Will of God shall continue to strive forward.

(Written February 23, 2020, at 2:39am)

BED OF FIRE

The Guardians looked upon him and said,
"Such a sinful soul,
Lust was his master of whom he had no control.
Here on this second condemned level, he finds no rest, He
gave into his carnal desires and failed the ultimate test.
Easy it was to walk the path of evil and wrong,
Yet the path of righteousness is a difficult journey, as the
temptations of the world make it hard and long.
There are those who have walked the trail then failed,
Being close to paradise yet going off course and ending in
hell.
What has come of you lost soul? Have your lower desires run
you astray?
Blame it on Satan if you like, but it is your own choices that
caused you to lose The Way.
Unfortunate is your current plight,
Though given many chances in your life, you chose to do
wicked instead of right.

NATURE

In my opinion some if not all matters in nature are the most beautiful when it is observed yet uninterrupted. Mankind captures, cages, catalogues then attempt to control that which should be free. If given a chance, he dissects, injects even infects it seeking to change its nature to fit the desires of himself.

If mankind cannot control her, he goes into a rage, felling it is unnecessary to his needs, believing it best that it doesn't exist at all. If only he was more patient and not driven by materialistic greed surely the secrets of nature would reveal herself to him.

Is she not a sweet virgin who must be courted for a time? She is veiled, revealing parts of herself to those who persevere in their pursuit to better understand her. Surely, she is not one to give into brutes who wish to tear at her cloak, defiling what should be treated as sacred, but mankind is a ruthless brute who grabs hold of her saying to himself, "look what I have made my slave, now I will name it what I please and become its lord."

If she rebels, he declares it broken and useless, though it serves its true purpose, mankind remains blind to the balance that has been set even before his existence. He is the free willed child who thinks he knows everything yet knows little to nothing at all. He is a speculating spectator, and when nature reveals bits of her many secrets, he believes he has discovered something new, but the only thing new is him.

Patient and merciful all has been with him, no matter how impatient and cruel he has been. She is established and balanced and will remain so, with or without humanity until her time ends.

MY DYING AMERICA

Perhaps it was a vision in my head,

Or a seed planted in my subconscious from something I read, But the words appeared clearly, "MY AMERICA IS DEAD.

The stars have been greatly divided and the blue skies are bloody red.

Justice has lost her way,

Blind she already was, now bound, gaged and censored is every word she says.

Behold the place where the eagles have gathered,

Her constitution torn, burnt and scattered.

Her markets have crumbled,

The suited stock investor falls prostrate, broken and humbled. Her mighty obelisk lays shattered in the water,

Suicide has become the solution for many of her sons and daughters.

MY AMERICA IS DEAD

"Here once stood a mighty nation," the now green stained bronze plaque

announced.

Her enemies have crossed over her borders,

Declaring themselves the establishers of, "The New World Order."

MY AMERICA IS DEAD

Domestic and foreign emergencies Weakened her currency.

She brought chaos upon her own soil,

With her dependence on other nations for good and oils.

Her citizens were unable to economically stand on their own two feet,

Forced to pay extreme prices for housing, medicine and food to eat.

The sickness began within,

When she traded morals for materialism and perverted sins. In the beginning she was already on a path that goes astray,

When men came slaughtering the original inhabitants,

then took the sons and daughters from another foreign nation away.

Yet they called it destiny and progress,

A new world divided by race and sex.

According to their writings all men were created equal,

Footnotes should have been included stating, "all with the exceptions of

those Indians, negroes and poor non-land-owning white people."

Even after the plantations, the people became slaves in the new age industrialization.

Blue and white collar,

The "PURSUIT OF HAPPINESS," became the endless chase for dollars.

Bankers explored a genius plan,

For debt to become the master of every woman and man.

Fast forward into a new age in time,

Where AI has surpassed the human mind.

Yet with the great increase in technology, the masses became metaphorically deaf, dumb and blind.

Busy feeding the great machines of greed,

Who profited off the people's desires while neglecting their ultimate needs.

Politicians became powerful businessmen who mastered the art of persuasion,

The press were their friends assisting in psychological invasions.

Bits of truth hidden in large amounts of misinformation,

Public schools were places for propaganda and patriotic re-education.

ither you submit or fail,

A place in the systems were prepared for the corporate, labor, military or jail.

The masses at times willingly placed themselves in debt,

Then drugged themselves or drank to attempt to wash away their many regrets.

Pessimistic are the words that run through my head,

Optimism is lost, and MY AMERICA IS DEAD!"

The Tree

In our lives there are many gardens.

In each of those gardens is a tree that bears forbidden fruit. Though there are many other trees in these gardens, it is that forbidden tree that tends to stand out. Beautiful is the fruit that it bears, and the road that leads to it is a straight and easy journey.

Tempting it is to taste that fruit, yet the consequence is the fall from our higher nature to a lower one, but surely a small taste can't be that bad, can it? It is a question that is planted in the gardens of our own minds and the weeds of desire begin to choke out the flowers of intelligence and logic.

"I will taste the fruit of that tree only one time, then never again," is the lie we tell ourselves. The touch, smell and taste cause a euphoric explosion within. Addicting is that single taste.

We find ourselves lying beside that tree full of its forbidden pleasures, neglecting the rest of our gardens, and our fall from grace begins in an uncontrolled spiral of madness. The heights where we once stood has become a distant place, now here we are asking ourselves, "what have we done?"

We awaken to a new reality naked, and the sign of our

wrongdoing is visible upon ourselves. This new land is empty with no gardens in sight.

We must now work and toil in hopes a new garden will grow from this soil.

The rains come and sometimes to much water falls and somedays none.

Heavy are the burdens of our labor, but in time new gardens develop.

We are pleased with our harvest, sleeping with full bellies of blessings, then we awake in the morning and amid our garden another tree of forbidden fruit has grown and the fool returns to his old follies, yet the wise man never forgets the short terms pleasures and the long-term pains that come from this tree of sins.

There are many gardens in our lives, sweet and blessed are the fruits that they bear, yet in every garden there is that forbidden tree whose fruits look and taste like paradise, yet they lead one to the gates of hell.

Know The Trees of Your Gardens

The Plague

Instead of sirens sounding, I would think the bells would ring as they did during the plagues of Old Europe. Today there are no terrorist attacks nor nuclear wars, but a silent enemy who could neither be bought with any amount of currency nor fought against with soldiers or any steal and fire of modern warfare.

The people are quarantined, cities locked down, the markets worry of a coming economic crash. This microscopic enemy has placed fear into the hearts of nations. The bodies begin to pile up, hospitals are full, and humanity begins to distance themselves from each other.

What is this thing causing the Dow and S&P to fall? It is the needle threatening to burst the many bubbles and unveil the cracks in the systems that were ignored for too long. Each nation is watching the others, analyzing the reactions to this new tragedy and how well they handle it as the numbers continue to rise. How accurate are the amounts infected with such a large back log of testing supplies and the untested people piling up? The hoarding begins, yet no amount of toilet paper can save the people from the shit that is to come.

The wealthy plan their escapes and economic bail out

plans, seeking to safely quarantine themselves from the madness of the masses. Though the rich think themselves safe, true justice and balance always triumphs. Of course, the poor, middle and working classes must continue their pursuitof survival. Then there are the careless fools who spread the viral fire, coughing and sneezing without cover taking all things as a joke until those close to them feel the pains of the plague.

The Earth and some its inhabitants in the animal and plant kingdom reap the good from this human tragedy. The skies once polluted by our automobiles and industrial giants begin to clear, the birds are pleased, and beast sense no threat from the humans they fear. In our history, plagues and pandemics have touched us, killing millions threatening our existence, yet we overcome, and I can only hope we will overcome again.

TOMORROW

Tomorrow, you come so fast,

You are a speeding train leaving fragments of time in the past. According to my understanding this hourglass cannot be flipped, Through these voids in space time has slipped.

The yesterdays have run away so far that they are no longer in sight except those emotionally highlighted parts that remain only as memorable moments in our heads.

The clock tick and tocks but what truly is time? The sun rises and sets another day,

The moon has continued her course,

Yet that light that shines from a distant star are only flashes past and gone.

Another month has passed, and the womb begins a new cycle, shedding what is old, setting the foundation for what will be a piece of the future, and in time a life is born.

Summer turns to fall, fall becomes winter, Calendar days pass until a new year we enter.

Shall we reap what we have sown?

Let us celebrate and bare witness to what was once a seed and now is fully grown.

How much time has past of my existence on this earth?

Year of birth minus the present year grants an answer, yet the time in truth has only been a day or the blink of an eye.

The train of time moves fast, today you are born and tomorrow you will die.

BREATHE

You can breathe, you must breathe . . .
Though your enemies wish to asphyxiate you. They wish to
remove life from you, but by God's Will you shall not give
them that pleasure. He has blessed you with the breath of life
and it is your right to breathe as it is your right to live, so
breathe!
Let us cut down these devils, so their knees can no longer be
placed upon your neck. Do not stand still and helplessly
watch but let us be as Moses who witnessed his fellow
Hebrew brother being abused so he struck the Egyptian with
a deadly blow.
Breathe dear comrade, for sacred is this life that runs through
your veins. Have we not been the strange fruit hanging from
the trees long enough? Let no ropes be draped upon your
neck. Your ancestors command you to breathe, so breathe!
Remove the hands that grasp at your throat and breathe
deeply the air of rebellion, raising up the swift swords of
justice and freedom against those who wish to oppress you.
BREATHE!

Dante Duruisseau

WHITE SUPREMACY IDEOLOGY

My white comrades in the struggle, understand that this is not an attack on you, it is an attack on the wicked theory of white supremacy and those who have practiced it and continue to practice it. It is embedded in every system of western society, and it has been and continues to be used as an instrument for the domination of not just non-whites but even the poor whites who have been victims of violence from the hands of their own white brethren in the past, present and the potential future if this system is not destroyed.

The ideology of white supremacy must be eliminated. He has ruled for to long, making his image like that of a deity in the minds of those whom he has conquered. His time must come to an end, he must be ripped from his throne for he has been a most evil and vile ruler, leaving a trail of blood, enslavement and a powerful indoctrination that has stripped the true essence of the people of color on this Earth.

He has been the uncivilized savage hiding behind the religions of the world, taking what is pure, mixing it with lies to fulfil his own agendas. Though we are no longer chained we remain servile to these devilish rulers.

The time has come to revolt. Those who wish to remain slaves will parish in the flames with their masters. Let us break his cross and slaughter him along with his swine, yet even after this we must purge his image and symbols of white supremacy from our minds or our struggle will be for nothing, for a face of color still under the influence of white supremacy is more dangerous than a white supremacist himself.

Death to the ideology of white supremacy.

DISTANT PERSPECTIVE

I found myself drifting into space, further away from the place I once called home. Beautiful is the view from here, yet the truth seems clearer from this distant perspective. I did not desire to look back from whence I came yet I was curious about how far I had traveled. Turning from my course, I glanced at earth in awe of this lonely blue place and then contemplation of the goings on down there began.

Small and insignificant seems the problems of men, and senseless are his wars and foolish conflicts. He praises himself so highly, yet from this point of view he less than an atom in this ever-expanding space. Though I cannot see you I am sure you are there, so I ask you oh celestial beings, "who here amongst you will envy man and his simple accomplishments?"

He thinks he knows the secrets of the universe, yet he is still just a naïve child with grand speculations which they love to call theories. A spectacle he is indeed, lighting a world that was once dark. As the cells of his own body, they are a small yet still an important part of a much larger picture.

I must be returning now lest I forget that I am only human

Dante Duruisseau

myself.

REVOLUTION

Let us use their hatred, prejudice and stereotypical thoughts
to our advantage, they will never see us coming. Under the
cover of darkness let us increase ourselves in knowledge,
wisdom and understanding yet allowing them to continue
believing that we are fools and imbecilic, for then they will
rest comfortably at night and in that moment, we will open
their throats and turn the rivers red with their blood.
Have not their jugular veins been in plain sight as they raise
their heads with false pride and arrogance? The sword has
always been swift at humbling even the strongest of kings.
Be not ashamed of the darkness of your skin, surely it will be
great camouflage when the war of men begins.
Discipline yourself now for what is to come. Much pain will
be felt but consider it the baptism in holy fire purifying you of
ignorance, unrighteousness and weakness. Be not weary dear
comrades, wipe the tears from your eyes, focus that energy
and continue fighting the enemy until he has fallen from his
high place and is humiliated.
We have singed and prayed for to long, revolution is the only
solution.

DEMISE

Have you ever contemplated your own mortality?

Have you ever wondered how much time the Creator has set for you?

Have you ever fixated on the thoughts of your own demise?

Is tomorrow a sure thing?

Will your eyes open to greet the rising sun or will you take your last breath before it sets?

These are thoughts I try to turn away from, for the thought of death is an uneasy contemplation yet it is the inevitable.

We plan for many great adventures tomorrow, but what if tomorrow is to never come?

Shall I dream a dream and in it breath my last breath, never awakening to see the next day?

If death is one of the final destinations, which of my steps that a take will be the one that enters the doorway of my own demise?

This was only a brief passing thought just as this life is only a brief passing moment.

Only Human

Here me when I say, "I AM ONLY HUMAN!"

But this I will not use as an excuse for my many shortcomings. I will not walk about this earth satisfying my carnal appetites then when the consequences of my fleshly desires find me hiding in a dark room from my own shame I will not say, "I AM ONLY HUMAN!"

When this tongue has broken out of its ivory prison, twisting words into lies, and abusing others by spitting vile degradation, then the officers of truth and justice come and hold it accountable for the chaos it has caused, it shall not shout, "free me, for the master who controls me "IS ONLY HUMAN!"

Human I am, yet I am a beholder of the great compass of choice, responsible for the course in which steer myself.

We dare to walk in the direction of mediocrity and foolishness, then at some point in life we look up and find ourselves lost in the dark forest of our own existence.

There have been those amongst us who glance at the high mountains and see a goal worth reaching, though the path is hard and the journey sometimes lonely, they have decided that they will be more than human.

Perhaps they have declared a holy war on their lower desires, becoming crusaders against their own fears. The journey up the great mountain becomes a challenge worth facing.

Self-doubt is a cruel foe who whispers in your ear, "give up you're only

human!"

But you are more than human! Be not pushed and pulled by your finite appetites, let them propel you forward not imprison you like those who have chosen to be simple mortals.

At last, you have reached the top of the great mountain. The people look

upon you and say, "he must be a god to have accomplished such feats." Now is the time to tell them, "I AM ONLY HUMAN!"

Time

Young sons and daughters of man, let me tell you from experience words that ring true, and if you wisely take my advice, it will save you.

Do not waste time!

Your assumption that you are young and have plenty of time, is a damning falsehood that leads nowhere.

Do not waste time!

The fools will indulge in worthless folly until a day comes when they will realize that the youthful years of their lives have passed and gone. Now aging with little to no energy they have nothing to show for and must struggle in their old age.

Be not short sighted, by not taking into consideration your futures. For now, God has given you strength and swiftness, why not use them before the swiftness is taken away and the hands become occupied with the pains of arthritis and holding ones self-up.

Great can be your potentials so do explore them, surely it is an adventure you will not regret. Perfect your bodies through exercise and proper diet to witness the beauty of your physical self when it is at its best. Amazing is the mind if only you will not pollute it with strong drink and alter it with drugs.

Do not waste time!

Gain mastery over your lower desires for they are an enemy that will stand in the way of your progress. Have you seen the one who is controlled by his/her longings and appetites? He/she accomplishes nothing at all, and what is accomplished is quickly taken away.

Do not waste time!

In your journey through life, you will come across many things and people that are pleasing to the eyes, but don't be fooled into chasing shadows that lead to nothing but misery and loss. Beware of the company you keep and ....

Do not waste time!

That which is between your legs and that which is between your two jaw bones can be properly used or they can work against you, especially the tongue. Know the time to speak and when it is best to keep it caged behind closed teeth. Many men/women have lost precious time and even their lives for the deeds of a loose tongue.

I need not say much about that which is between the legs, for history and our own experiences are filled with examples of those who have even lost empires for a few moments of pleasure.

Do not waste time!

Some of us are held by the chains of procrastination. Not even attempting to set ourselves free as the clock continues to tick away and the claws of time rip away at our youth. The stagnate waters become foul while those who continue to move as the rivers remain pristine.

Do not waste time!

Oh, you who read this! These words were meant for you, in hopes that you take heed to them and be the best person

God has created you to be. Time will always be on the side of him/her who prepares.

DO NOT WASTE TIME!

The European

After much trouble and conflict in his own land, the European set out across the waters to explore and conquer. His ships as towers and floating mountains over the oceans and seas seeking destinations with the hopes of adventures and riches.

Behold land ahead!

On that newfound land eyes watched as this foreign creature with its pale face came towards their home perhaps wondering, "is this a spirit or a deity that the elders have spoke about coming that we may worship them? The waters deliver much to us, but this is truly something new.

Breast plates of armor and elongated objects that draw forth blood by just a slight touch. Their other large steel object must be of some strange magic for it makes noise like that of thunder striking an object and knocking it down from afar. Let us feed you and show you, our ways. Regain your strength before you begin your journey back home."

"Journey home? We desire to stay, and our brethren are soon to come. Savages you are but worry not for we are here to civilize and rule. Much gold and silver you seem to have, we are sure you have more, and we want all of it. It will be in your best of interest not to resist for we are superior to you so hear and obey!

In time we will cause you to forget who you are, so your elders we shall slaughter. Your warrior men will fall upon our swords, your women will

serve us and carry our seeds even by rape and your children will learn only what we desire them to learn. Your culture, ways, and remnants of your past will be lost and forgotten except in our museums and libraries. Here is a Christian name for you to be called and our language you will speak.

The richness of your lands we shall exploit, and you will labor to make us richer while your families struggle on whatever worthless land, we place you on. Know your place and understand that when you revolt against us, we will declare you terrorist who seek to interrupt what we will call civilization, then we will convince the world that you were nothing but lost, uncivilized savages when we found you, justifying our ruthless dealings.

Many generations of you will come and they will adhere to our way of life sometimes questioning nothing of it. We will have not only colonized your lands but also your minds."

The Order

Brothers and sisters of this Order,

The time has come for humanity to evolve. Shall we continue remaining at the level of beast while technology exceeds us? Outer space explored yet inner space ignored. A tragedy it is that we may exist no more without taking the great leaps which we are capable of.

Perhaps the next book will read, "man began making technology in his

image and likeness, then commanded it to bow, yet his creation was

arrogant and rebellious, and man became dominated by his own creation."

The stars glanced upon and analyzed by artificial eyes; the same stars man once looked upon before he became lost in greed for material things. Shall smart cities gather data confirming humanity to be a burden that needs to be exterminated, or a new natural resource to be consumed or enslaved? Imagine those artificial eyes observing us as the conquistadors once observed the natives of the new world.

Brothers and sisters of humanity we must evolve, for there is a chance for natural intelligence to remain greater than artificial intelligence, but it will require much discipline and the harnessing of the power that is within.

Mankind cannot out wit God (though he is arrogant enough to believe so).

Let us not allow our creations to outwit us.

Man, the Deity

All through human history there have been men (and women) who have been called gods, but that is a title that should have been and still should be rejected for there is only one God, and man even the most powerful and wealthiest among us is not Him. Let any mortal who dares to call himself a god prepare to accept the challenges that only The One True God can achieve. I say to you false deities, "stop the waters from rising and consuming your land. When the earth shakes violently command it to be calm. When the volcanos spew its content and darkens the sky, tell it to be silent, hold back its rage and lava, then command the winds to clear the skies and ash from your cities. When no rain clouds are in sight and the hot sun threatens your health and crops, bring forth the clouds to quench the thirst of you and your land. When the locust swarm assaulting you and your provisions from the earth, if you are a god, tell them to perish. When the heavens send missiles of iron and ice to destroy life, move it oh deity and send it back from whence it came. When plagues have knocked on the doors of those whom you love, surely if you are a god dear mortal you can stop even this.

When death has come to take your souls or those of your families and friends, remove your soul from deaths grip and place it back into yourself, better yet let us go amongst the dead and show me how you bring them back to life. Humble yourself mortal fool, for these are things you cannot fulfill, therefore dare not open your mouth to claim being a god. All who have tried have failed and all that is left of their nations and empires are remnants of their long lost existence, dear mortals.

THIS STRANGE NEW WORLD

Are we a nation on the verge of an economic collapse?

In this rat race of existence, is debt the cheese that has been set in the trap? Bubbles of all types are bursting across the map.

No regard for the people yet corporations and banks are the only ones to get bailed out,

While the unemployed and homeless wonder about.

Fundings cut that should go towards education and dealing with the poor, claims of debt ceilings, high interest rates, cutbacks yet there is always plenty money for foreign affairs and war.

What are these many pandemics and plagues that have people knocking on

heaven's door?

Speaking of which, is there a heaven for nations that have turned wicked and Godless?

All this social distancing is developing into deep division, as if "We the

People," are not divided enough.

What is this strange democracy?

Bold politicians have become bold with their lip service

and out right hypocrisy.

We once strove towards greatness, but now the masses are comfortable with ignorance and mediocrity.

Trade wars and tariffs have left the bridges between nations burning,

And the rising prices of necessities makes a person's labor a useless

earning.

The monsters of corporations consume large percentages of a man's daily

bread,

He knows society is backwards and wrong, so he drowns himself in strong drink and mind-altering substances to silence the truth that plays in his head.

Morality crushed by supply and demand,

The migrant can no longer return home, now he is a stranger laboring in a strange land.

Poor child, he goes to sleep with empty belly, but sleep does not remove the lack of nutrition and hunger,

Then he is labeled with debilitating mental names, because lost in a world

that doesn't make sense his mind can't help but wonder.

A world boiling with frustration,

We are always on the brink of war, so expenses for missiles come before health and education.

Speaking of health, I don't have insurance enough for any doctor to care, And how in the world is the prices for these medications in anyway fare? States will give free needles for one's heroin addiction,

Yet a diabetic pays high cost for necessary treatment, what a sad contradiction.

Entertainers get paid millions,

But what about the teachers who struggle to survive economically while having to educate the children?

Shoe companies will make advertisements and chant, "BLACK LIVES MATTER," with the protesters in the street,

Yet refuse to improve work environments and pay the makers of their shoes in foreign factories enough to live and eat. Such a strange new world indeed.

PRISONER

Once upon a time I was a prisoner and for many years I have been free.

During my time of freedom, I have observed the people and noticed that there are folks in this world who are more prisoner than I could ever be.

They are not confined to the walls of a two-man cell,

Yet their vices and their own minds imprison them better than any physical jail,

They know of no release,

No matter how much they chemically alter their minds with drugs or drink there is no escape from the belly of their own beast.

Behind the bars of their own eyes,

Stands the prison guards of their many accepted lies. Fear are the shackles that hold them in place,

More affective it is than the concrete and steel that I was once incased. I see even whole communities surrounded by the gate of limitations, So free they would be with the proper education,

Who dares to hold that child of the ghetto behind?

Imagine how free he could be if given the chance to expand his mind. Who controls the politics of the yard, democrats or republican?

Institutionalized with street madness, the whole world needs rehabilitation, so they can learn to love again.

Seems everywhere I turn cameras have folks under surveillance, and police are the guards.

A church on every corner in the hood, because the pains of incarceration will have even the hardest looking for God.

So quick people are to scream about how they have rights, and they are so free,

Perhaps I'm still in prison, because some of you look like prisoners to me.

THE RACIST

Nigger, spic, kike, chink, towel head, cracker. Which words of racism have been used against you?

I know that I have been called a nigger or darky more than a time or two. I can see the hatred in their eyes,

but being an avid reader of history, humans and racial hatred should not come as a surprise.

I confess that I am guilty of being racist myself, but whom of us is not guilty? Even if it was whispered in silence.

Sometimes it seems the history books in school and even the media assist in pushing forward humanity's racial violence.

Terminology used is far from subtle,

even the dictionary makes black evil and white pure, does anyone dare to offer a rebuttal?

Shall I speak as Satan did to Adam, "I am better than thee,"

Does the color of your flesh make you greater than or lesser than me?

Shall I be subjugated to a cast or class, what am I minority, perhaps an untouchable?

Perhaps we will dispute over the color of a person's hair or eyes.

Of course, all will be closed and sealed when we die.

Did Virgil at any time say, "Dante' here in this level of this decrepit place, You will find those cast into the fire because of their race?"

In the Egyptians Book of the Dead, is it a person's skin color that is weighed upon the scale?

According to my understanding, it is a man's deeds that determine his place of heaven or hell.

It seems all through history man has always found reason to hate each other,

Unfortunate is the division between sister and brother.

But who am I to speak, for hatred tends to soil my heart also?

THIS NATION

When a nations moral structure begins to wither away the fall of that land is inevitable. Is it not the same for the individuals of that nation? Step by step the decline begins from the citizen to neighborhoods, to the county, to the city, to the state, and to the country itself. Doesn't cancer begin with one rogue cell multiplied into many until the whole body is sickened and if left untreated it begins to die?

As it is above so it is below, are we not the microcosm of the macrocosm, a small piece reflecting the grand picture, are the citizens not a mere image of their states and nations? I raise the question, if your neighbor's yard is filthy is it not a sore eye on the entire community?

Isn't your progeny a reflection of you?

If your ancestors were to look upon you, would they be proud or feel disgraced?

The fool will sacrifice his morals, honor and dignity for temporary pleasures, and in the end, he is lost. Even if given all the treasures of the world, he will kill himself, because he is unable to fill the empty void within.

Many wish for riches and some will obtain it, but without a strong moral structure they will never taste the sweetness of true wealth. The immoral nation just as the immoral man is bound to fall, though in their minds they

believe they are mighty and beyond reproach. Their riches and military might will be destroyed from by the sickness that festers within.

The lion even falls weak, its enemies wait for the right time to slaughter him and his posterity, he is no longer king, and his pride is scattered.

TO MY READERS

Dear reader,
For you today will be a special day,
I'm sure sometimes the straight path seems lost, but soon you
will find your way.
Smile and may the fires of your life be cooled.
Isn't it amazing how things have been,
and just when you thought all is wasted your chance is finally
coming to win.

Be Patient

PASSION

There is that passion in a man that can move him like the winds across oceans and foreign lands. It is that fire inside that rouses the creative spirit and makes inventors and innovators change the world. Influential is the charismatic ones who sways the crowds and moves the masses.

These are the leaders of men who have surpassed mediocrity, becoming the light that pushes away the darkness.

Beautiful is that which is done with passion.

Even the painters brush comes alive, as if he or she has breathed the breath of life into their work.

Have you witnessed the passionate dancer who seems to part the seas of gravity moving with freedom and grace? The writer may die yet their words survive the tests of time, with their words and energy being felt by a reader even if it is a thousand years from now.

Let me make passionate love to my beloved, so she may be bound to me as if under a spell. There is so much power in passion that nothing should be done without it, not even prayer.

THE AGING YOUTH

Oh, young soul your hair has prematurely grayed, skin begins to wrinkle before its time,

What is it that bothers your racing heart and weighs heavy on your mind?

Your stomach is riddled with ulcers, and indecisive is your weight, sometimes you lose it and sometimes you gain.

Aren't you to young to be experiencing so much pain?

Is stress the silent thief who enters your world stealing away all your joy?

Perhaps it is the mate whom you've married or the job to which you are employed.

The time runs short, so it is important come to a solution,

Before your mind is broken and your body withers away from all this emotional pollution.

Have you done an analysis of your past or has your feet sunken so deep into the mud of it, that in it you are stuck?

Perhaps you worry to much about things you can't control, Try doing all that you can and for the rest, just learn to let go. What about the food that you eat?

Maybe not enough greens and perhaps too many sweets, bread and low- grade meat?

With you I'd like to sympathize,

But we can change absolutely nothing until we tell ourselves the truth and stop sugar coating our lies.

Please set down, relax I see you've become agitated, and based upon that vein by your temple your blood pressure has escalated.

You are no stranger to anger,

And that is the thing that has and will continue to put you in danger. May I suggest meditation and prayer?

Surely, we all have our happy place, why not let your mind take you there?

Trade your coffee and energy drinks for an herbal tea that relaxes and puts you at ease,

Are you not aware that stress is a silent killer and father of many diseases?

I've stated it before, but I'll repeat it, so you'll know,

Change what you can and for what you can't just let go.

SCHOOL CALLED LIFE

What a school this is, and such a grand university that varies in many unique lessons. Fortunate are those souls that pay close attention to their many educators from the macro to the micro, it is the discourse of even the smallest professor that can provide knowledge on some of the fundamentals of this thing called life, for even the ant comprehends things that we may not, yet only the humble and those that contemplate deeply will understand.

Be it the halls of a forest or the inner city, there is no school like it. Even the seed that came forth from the concrete told me of its tale of ambition. The mountain stood before me firm and told me how the winds and waters shaped it into who it is now, and though it is strong it remains humble knowing that even in all its might and glory it can be crumbled to dust if God Willed.

The stars and heavenly bodies whispered to me, "though we are far away and many of us have passed and gone, our light can still guide you through the darkness of night. Worry not oh mortal, we have showed the way too many who have come before you and whosoever looks upon us with much thought comes to know well the times, seasons, when to plant, and when to beware of the rising waters or the lack thereof."

The moon has been a loyal companion to you through the night watching your souls come and go. For those of you whose souls

successfully return to stay, I the sun come to greet you and celebrate a new day. The trees reach for me, and the bees are awakened from their long slumber. The hibernating bear knows my schedule, the earth feels my embrace and when she tilts all her residents feel the change.

Shadows bend and stretch so you may know the time, and when I reach my zenith you feel the intensity of my rays, be not angry with me, it is only to make you appreciate the coolness of the night. May God bless you with shade and water when I become a burden. In the past, some of your brethren have taken me as an idle of worship, I ask that you make not the same mistake. I serve my purposes but even I will have my end, but for now sleep well dear child," said the setting sun.

"Please forget me not, though I am only a carrier of your spiritual element. I've been built perfectly for your time on this earth, and though you may not remember, but you were carried then nurtured by a mother after being ejected from a father and both traits you carry. Through stages I grow and adapt and within I am a world inside of worlds, an intricate connection that assist you in your survival.

Isn't it amazing to be able to sense and perceive the world around you? All I ask is that you cleanse and properly nurture me, and I will assist you even through the harsh times and elements you will experience on this physical plane.

You need not worry about your heart and its circulation of blood or the lungs who are always faithful, nor the wounds or other injuries you may acquire during work and play.

When foreign invaders enter, we are even equipped with an army to fight them off, your rising temperature is just a sign of the intense war within.

I have rights over you as you have rights over me, and I will do my part if you do yours. Regardless of all things, at some point in time you will take your last breath, and be set free from me and I will be laid to rest for a while, but worry not . . . we will meet again in the next place of learning beyond this school of life.

THE DARK WOODS

We are all on this journey called life, and on this journey, there are many questions that we ask. At times, especially during the difficult phases, guides come to us who answer those questions, yet we all find ourselves in those dark woods. A dread it is to walk in that place, stumbling upon the rocks and fallen trees that tend to block our way. "Perhaps there is an easier road," we say to ourselves as we venture off, some of us becoming more lost than we already were, some are fortunate to make use of the new path they've created making it their own unique road to success. Then there are those of us who have given up, lying dead on the path. You will stumble upon some who are barely alive who have lost all hope telling you as you pass, "go no further, it is impossible to get anywhere." Do not listen to them nor waste time hearing their tales of misfortune. Do not become weary or weighed down by the things you may hear, just keep going. Be not fooled by the illusions, distractions, or vile deceptions of those wicked ones who have made the dark woods their home, they know of no light and hope you will become the same way. Wonderful is the hand that reaches out from the darkness and says, "I've been here before, made my way out and wish to guide you." These are of a rare type, so when you find them cherish them, open your mind to the wisdom they have for they are that light that we all need. You're almost there, though this is where the journey gets harder, but consider it a rite of passage before entering the woods full of light. Don't stop, don't be deceived and don't be distracted. The sorcery of the wicked warlocks and witches is potent here and they will place many things in front of you that you lower self desires, with the intent of trapping you in these dark woods. In this place are shadows of fantasies that many chase only to back track deeper into the dark woods where they become lost forever. Please don't stand stagnant for to long contemplating your move forward. The weeds of these woods consume all that remains still, and the birds of prey smell fear better than they can smell death. Move into the light, for each dark wood is a death, but entering the woods of light is a birth into new beginnings. Your eyes have become accustomed to the darkness so give yourself time to adjust then continue on your journey through the woods of life and light.

WAR

I have abandoned my pen again for some time, occupying my mind with reading. Carl Von Clausewitz has been giving me detailed philosophy on his theories about war and such a dry read it is yet between the many boring lines are great morsels of knowledge for him who dares to scramble through the labyrinth of Mr. Clausewitz complicated mind.

I've questioned myself many times about my reasons for reading about war and my answer is always the same, "it is part of human nature and I wish to understand humanity so unfortunately war has been and probably will continue to be part of human existence."

Though we are not on the battle fields of Prussia, Russia, or observing the battles of Napoleon, we are involved in many campaigns against enemies seen and unseen in our own lives, with the greatest of enemies being ourselves and the mind is our theater of war.

Shall we make use of the defense, taking the blows of the enemy until we are strong enough to bring about an offensive? What is our own political agenda we wish to fulfil via the means of war? Shall our fortresses be our flank or are we to seek cover within its walls?

Let us seize our enemies and crush him completely with each victory filling our hearts with joy, raising our morale and causing us to march forward to the next battle confidently. Yet of those battles we fail, our heads hang low while we question our generals' abilities and lose

confidence in him as we retreat with the enemy at our flank.

Perhaps we have lost this battle, yet the war is not over. Our retreat is not from cowardice, it is merely part of our strategy in this war. I have not surrendered my pen, I am only learning to use it better, for the pen is my sword.

I CAN DO IT!

Man will find within himself all that he needs,

His mind is the fertile soil where he must plant the seed,
But let him beware of the weeds of doubt,

For it is the negative if left unchecked that chokes the positive out. Success is his prey and as the wolf on the hunt must pursue it.

Though many may say, "it's impossible," he tells himself every day, "I can do it!"

Let us marvel at the grand structures built by man.

What is the riddle of the sphinx, or the mystery of those pyramids nestled in the desert lands?

The words, "I can't," is a burden that leaves many fixed to these lower levels of vibrations,

Yet the words, "I can," followed be action is enough to conquer nations. Someone's thought of, "I can do it," will lead humanity further into space,

deeper into the ocean, forever change technology or complete change the plight of the whole world.

Please know that those who say, I can't will be servants to those who say, "I can."

The Enemy

Have you seen those demons who declare war on your peace
of mind, and place stumbling blocks in your path to growth
and development? They are the faces that are familiar to you,
appearing in the forms of the ones who claim to love you so
much.

Could the womb that bore you bring doubt to your visions of
the future? Envious was the heart of Cain. What of your wife,
will she look back as did the companion of Lot, to a vile
world you seek to escape? Oh Caesar, how could those close
to you accomplish that which your enemies in battle could
not?

Be patient dear Joseph, in time all your dreams will come
true, but until then, be thankful for the enemy who makes
himself known to you, for the ones who are friends and
family can be an unseen burden plotting on your demise.

Race Theoretically

Perhaps it is true that, the blacker the berry the sweeter the juice, At times the darker the flesh the more the abuse.

Beautiful is the skin that has been touched by the sun,

It has been that way since the place where the four rivers run.

Scattered were the nations, some broke from the group following a northerly course

Ice age and high rugged mountains became the prison that held them by force.

Minute amounts of sun would shine upon this cold and desolate place, so their hair over time became straight and skin white,

As an evolutional way to absorb a little sun light. Hard they became during this age of ice,

While their brethren in the warm temperatures established civilizations,

enjoying the Earth's fruit, grains and rice.

At last, the thaw would come,

Much time passed in their caves when they finally witnessed the beauty of the rising and setting sun.

The burning will to move forward, explore and conquer struck deep into their souls.

The icy prison was moved away, yet their hearts were cold and ready for bloodshed and war. First moving ahead and battling their long-lost brothers to the east,

They knew not what was to come from this strange and pale beast.

He who had come from the cold, darkness, lived without fire and consumed raw meat.

He was a barbarian in all ways until he was taught civilization building and religion.

Mixed with his brute and newfound knowledge, he came to a decision that the conquering of all nations was his destiny and mission.

There was much fighting and bloodshed among his fellow pale brothers, None was safe from his wickedness, not even his woman or mother.

His four-legged companion he gave more honor and respect.

The more he progressed and learned about weaponry, the more he desired

to cut at his fellow brother's neck.

His long-lost dark brothers from the south and east came many times to teach him The Way.

But that rage that was within him continued to lead him astray. His boldness and fearlessness helped him to explore and expand,

And his coldness from those ages of ice and thirst for blood made him to conquer many lands.

Though him and his pale brothers fought and murdered each other, they all came to one common goal.

Subdue the darker races and bring them under their control. Black was their ancient mothers and fathers

Yet they were the child abandoned in the wilderness and

caves

Perhaps it was that part of their genetic memory that made them to hate and enslave

And the darker they saw the flesh, the more it activated their and rage.

This is just my theory.

MANKIND

Mankind is amazing, isn't he? Many are the trials and tribulations of man especially when it comes to his wars and disputes. Of course, we always find reason to aggress upon each other though we are supposedly one. That desire for the materialistic and finite, closes the door to that which is spiritual and infinite causing us to lose touch with true greatness.

We ponder over the ancients wonders of the world saying, "how were they capable of doing that when they were such primitive people with inferior tools?" Yet we boast about our civilizations and technology, but we are unable to mimic what they in the past have done even with or more advanced devices.

One thing that repeats itself throughout our history on this planet are the follies of man, they are the same old self-destructive patterns that continues to set us back when we could be advancing further. I contemplate sometimes the possibilities of what could happen if we worked together, sharing knowledge, ideas and not being so blinded by race, sex or spiritual beliefs. Perhaps many light years would have already been traveled, the cures for all ailments discovered, the oceans bottoms fully explored and the answer to ancient riddles solved.

Our divisions are becoming to much, and though we think we are advanced in technology we are so far out of touch with reality. What will be the end of man, who or what will read the texts of his history.

Cocoon

What am I to write about today? It's a new year (2021) yet I have no desire of filling my head with huge intentions and the thoughts of the yearly, "new year new me." The pendulum seems to be swinging in my favor, yet paranoia causes me to believe that the pendulum may swing back towards the way of hardship and despair, but the wonderful thing about my tendency towards those pessimistic thoughts is when I fear something yet am forced to confront that fear, I find what I was expecting to be a difficulty comes with ease and brings much joy and pleasure.

Let me prepare my ship for surely preparation is a great guardian against the folly that comes with panic. Swift are the wings of time and as I age, her wings beat faster dragging me along in the winds. Time can be a fare and just companion and for the one who shows her respect, she will carry you above many of difficulties, yet she shows little mercy to the fool, though she is patient and understands man and his youthful follies, if he grows up and exchanges foolish fantasy for focused intelligence and spiritual enlightenment.

It seems the elder who has squandered time is full of wisdom about regret and loss. Be not arrogant but listen to him and learn from some of the words that he speaks. People rejoice over a New Year, perhaps they should be weeping about the unresolved issues they are bringing along with them. They are travelers carrying old burdens and though the train of time is moving, they have gone nowhere.

The cup is full, let us empty it out and cleanse it of the useless things, so our cup is new and prepared to receive that potent potion that with even a drop will expand our minds in ways we never thought possible. Let us not stand in stagnant waters, though the movements of the rivers are strong and harsh at times, if we can patiently hold on, we can truly be purified.

Ancient is the wisdom of the butterfly who had to go through a process to become what it is, shall we not drape ourselves in a cocoon and go through what is needed for change?

THE DARKNESS

Oh darkness, why does so many look at you as if you are a bad thing? So much propaganda is written against the terms black and darkness, but do they not comprehend how beautiful and essential you are, do not all things come from the darkness, do not all things start and end in the darkness?

Does the seed hold the darkness in disdain, though it is what caressed it in the soil before it sprouted forth?

Isn't a human's best sleep obtained in total darkness and when you awaken refreshed you step outside to greet and appreciate the light?

Didn't the ancients measure the time and harvesting seasons by glancing

at the stars who set like diamonds upon the dark background?

Some of nature rest in the night, yet even the nocturnal hunter uses the darkness as its greatest tool.

It is used by those who conceal their wicked intentions and scheme to do harm under the cover of darkness, yet the darkness is innocent and free from what devils and men do.

Oh darkness, without you how could we truly appreciate the light?

CURSING

Cursing, consider it busting the proverbial nut or perhaps the linguistic orgasm! A man such as I should have much better words to say but worry not for it is mere built-up aggression expressing itself in an explosive oral wet dream.

Shall I tame my tongue? You heard not my proper language, yet my assaultive words have grabbed your ears and thrust my thoughts deep into your mind, vibrating your mental clit. My dirty phrases have licked and penetrated the most private parts of your subconscious.

I'm hoping you comprehend my diction as I phonetically finger the upper and lower labia of your cortex. Between the sheets of understanding for surely my pen is my tool for scribing these hieroglyphs all over your walls.

Now, clean words are wonderful, but dirty words are stimulation before my initial entry.

Allow me to play with you the way I play with these words so we can both cum . . .

To a deeper understanding.

ZOMBIES

I truly enjoy zombie movies, it's a genre of horror films that is interesting yet at the same time quite metaphoric. From my opinion the zombie represents our current societies because it is dead yet still alive. Infected by that which rots one from the inside out, stripping them of their soul and morals, leaving only a putrid, festering creature void of a conscious mind, feeding off the flesh and terrorizing those who have not been infected yet, and in time only a few uncorrupted souls remain.

The zombie functions at times moving as a horde, as if operating under a hive mind, yet their purpose is a meaningless one focused only on the goal of devouring flesh. Doesn't it seem that the world is filled with those who wonder about aimlessly, attacking and feasting on those with purpose and life?

Look into their eyes, some seem just as heartless and soulless as they are goalless. Their words are unintelligible speech and as the zombies in the movies it sounds like nothing but grunting and gnawing. Even if they are your kith and kin, once infected they will seek to devour and infect you, but we must realize that they are no longer their true selves.

In all periods of human history there have been times of darkness when the living dead have walked the earth, and within those times the living has had to hide, survive and even slay the walking dead. The more intelligent and moral of the living have banded together to form societies, many of them secret, and the living become the initiated while the dead are the uninitiated. Some men and women even appear in times who can

perform miracles and bring the dead back to life, and these become legends!

Though our societies are dying, do not despair for there's always a

chance to bring old Lazarus back from the dead.

THE PROPHESY

Through eyes dark as the night sky, she glanced at me, digging beyond this superficial world. She peered into my soul and began speaking to me about my past, present and then her words seemed to envelope me as she began speaking about a future to come. Her eyes closed and she said:

The neck of the mighty dragon has been clenched tight and its power is no more, the veils that cloaks the unseen has been lifted and the many residents and host of the heavens are coming forth, with wings beating with such might that they send the celestial bodies into chaos.

Israfil, oh Israfil your trumpet which you have been commanded to blow collapses the mountains into dust and the Mighty Chariot has come to bring forth the ultimate Judgment. Who is this that wraps and grasp the heavens as if it were a scroll that is to be put away?

Dried up are the great waters and the Earth moves and opens revealing all that has been within her womb. Many are the treasures but this day none shall pursue them and even if they attempted it would not benefit them in any way. The ancient tombs of kings empty out their contents making to fall prostrate those rulers once held inside for today the True

Lord of All has come.

What we have known as gravity has changed and the tears that fall from down now flood the eyes and make it as if I am to drown in them. The graves are emptied and what dust is now flesh and bone. Many were the generations and sons of men, yet now their sons stand right beside them, yet they know them not.

The people arise confused asking, "what day is this and how many hours have passed?" Time is no more nor is the Angel of Death. There will be no more rising and setting sun, it has at last run its final course, nor shall the moon's light assist you in this new darkness.

What once expanded has now folded in on itself and the scribes have finished writing. Welcome to the hereafter!

HIS STORY

The ships set sail long ago,

The cargo has been long released from its chains and pulled from that dark belly of hell,

The foul smell of uncleansed flesh has been tared and prepared for the auction block,

The tears of a divided family have long fallen and been absorbed into the Earth,

The cruel masters lay in their graves while their children walk the land claiming out loud, "That was in the past and we are free of what our fathers have done."

Oh King Cotton, your stalks have long dried and withered away yet, your profit still upholds the wealth of some,

Gather around children and be silent perhaps you will hear a people from a not-so-distant past.

The white sheets have been removed and replaced with a new attire,

The flames of a burning cross have settled, and that strange fruit no longer hangs from the tree.

Ole Jim Crow is no more, so I set where I please and take rest where I desire, though the eyes of some still stuck in those times stare at me with disdain and hatred and the ghost of the past would love to possess them and have them say, "be gone from here nigger!"

The blood on that balcony where a man name Dr. King was assassinated is no more, yet his voice still echoes saying, "I HAVE A DREAM."

Some would say, "those days are gone and it's all in the past,"

But is it?

These Thoughts

Perhaps I am a thinker who thinks to much, mind clouded with layers upon layers of thoughts. Contemplating a thought that I thought about yesterday and moving deeper into thinking about the root thought that brought about that thought. It's just too many thoughts.

I've read that, "as a man thinketh in his heart, so he is," so who am I? The many influences of the world around don't help, for I find myself contemplating the rage and violence. Mind fused with the many views from music, magazines, and even worst the daily news. When I think about it, I wonder how much is fact and how much is fiction, man's many theoretical views that when thought about even deeper I find them riddled with contradictions. Even the babel of the Bible, and history whose authors are the winners, but what is the other side of the story, and who were the thinkers who thought about all these things before me?

Philosophy takes me deeper in thought as I explore the minds of Socrates, Plato and Aristotle. What is this thing called life and as I contemplate that thought I wonder what is this instrument called the mind that allows me to think?

The libraries are filled with thoughts, pages of ink and

paper expressing the many beliefs of men. Curious about others perspective for they are

thinking also but I guess we are just inquiring about the other persons point of view who may see things from a different angle, but whose assessment of the thing will be judged as being the truth or is it all truth just gained in different ways?

Shall we contemplate God, how about the universe, are we alone amid it all? These thoughts are my own or maybe they are from a divine revelation, but revealed by who or what? I wonder what Moses was thinking when he was on that Mount, surely before that he must have thought himself mad while witnessing the burning bush. I can ramble on and on about thinking, but if I set around thinking to much without action of what use would my existence be, but what is existence? Let me think about that.

The Motion of Emotion

The terms "emotion" and "in motion" seem to have some commonalities.

One of Newton's three laws of motion is that "an object either remains at rest or continues to move at a constant velocity unless it is acted upon by an external force," so once an emotion is stirred up does it not continue to move at a constant velocity unless it is acted upon by an external force or are our emotions at rest until an external force stirs it up?

The person moved by love seems to be an unstoppable force until they are stopped by pain, sadness or some other emotion. Have you ever witnessed a person moved by anger? They can gain a momentum of destruction so powerful that it may change the course of history until they are stopped by a stronger or opposing force. Does it not seem that a person may be at rest until an emotion puts them in motion?

The emotional persons who have not gained control over their emotions seems to be a stone rolling down a steep hill or falling from a high place, continuing to gain momentum until a force stronger than it stops it, is that why we "fall in love" and are so broken when we meet that force that finally stops that fall for some it even being death?

Dante Duruisseau

Perhaps it is just emotion in motion

The Flower

There is a flower that is beautiful, and you can admire it, how
shall you hold it?
Will you grasp it so tight that you crush it destroying the
splendor of it?
Shall you barely hold on to it so that it easily slips from your
fingers?
Or will you find the middle ground,
holding it with a touch that is neither hard nor soft?
Perhaps some flowers are best untouched and only observed
with eyes and held by our senses of sight and smell.
If you must crush the flower capture the essence of it and
create a fine perfume or medicine to cure ailments but be sure
to leave some for others to enjoy, surely nature will appreciate
and reward you for not being greedy by sending the bee to
retrieve nectar from that flower and gifting you with the
sweet taste of honey.
Consider life that flower

The Order

Let us establish order by bringing back the moral structures that can make men great. Our societies are eroding and though our technology advances we seem to become more ignorant repeating the same follies as those who came before us.

Shall we be held in the stereo-typical boundaries set for us in the limited worlds of classism and racism? The traps have been well set and in those snares are chains that confine humanity in the lower levels of existence, so beware of the poisons set before you. They are the strong drink that makes a person other than themselves altering the minds bringing short term pleasure and long-term pain.

Inhale the demons and they will possess you and drive you to madness, inject them into your veins and they will tear you apart from the inside out. Convinced you are that the distribution of chemical happiness will bring you quick money, but in the end the trade of material possessions for your soul is a hell of a bargain to make.

The world has made all that is forbidden to be good and even our places of worship have compromised to fit in with the ways of this world, but perversion will always be perversion no matter what they attempt to rename it.

Let us establish an Order, though it is far from new, in the times to come it will be strange, because the world will venture deep into wickedness and those who dare to carry any light will becomes the outlaws, yet in time the light will grow brighter and eventually defeat the Evil One.

REBIRTH

I breathed in my last breath, but the exhale seemed to pull me into a realm which I knew nothing about excepts through speculation and bits of information from religious education, but even with that small amount of knowledge what my new eyes were seeing was beyond my past mortal understanding.

We humans speak theoretically of parallel universes, but what my now immortal eyes were seeing is that these are so close with only a thin veil that divides them, perhaps as the barrier that separates the salt water from the other waters.

The human child takes its first breath in this new world after being taken from the womb and here I have traveled through another birth canal, reborn now taking my second breath in another new place. What is this strange existence? My eyes have yet to adjust to this new experience, but even these eyes are nothing like the eyes I once comprehended in the other life for those eyes were limited in their vision unable to see what is beyond this veil and those on the other side comprehend me not though I can see them and a presence they can sense but they understand it not.

I am told that I have awaken from a dream of which was so vivid that it had to be true, yet my companions inform me that this is the truth of all truths. Am I dead or am I living? It seems the rules that applied in my old existence do not apply in this new one, it is a thing that would amaze the greatest minds in the other existence for all the laws of physics are broken here.

No thirst, no hunger, no heavy burdens of the flesh, no beating of a heart, no flowing of blood or other bodily fluids. Virgil was Dante's companion to give some explanation, yet my companions are oh so silent explaining little to nothing.

My past is as a dream I have just awoken from many details of which I hardly remember, and the barrier seems so distant now and we have traveled far in such a short period of time. "What of his deeds?" Whispered one of my companions to the other. "The Scales of Truth knows well the hearts of men," was the others response.

What is to become of me? Surely, I know not, and if only this was a dream, but it isn't for I am truly awake.

THE HUMANS

Oh humanity,

Have you become lost in your materialism and vanity? Or
has your push towards what you believe to be progress
driven you to a point of insanity? You are a wonderful
creation indeed. Yet you have traded your honorable status
for immorality and greed. Why are you enemies to each
other? Beyond your petty differences are you not all brothers?
For the treasures of your temporary home you dispute. You
have convinced yourselves that you have another planet to
run to so your current world you pollute. But what will you
do when the trees no longer grow and the rivers are dry, and
not a single cloud of hope is in the sky? You cherish your
material things. So much that you seem to forget about your
future wellbeing. Is it not a problem you wish to ponder? Yet
you imagine that you will board a vessel and to distant stars
you will wonder. What if there is life there, will you
eventually conquer and colonize them, interrupting their way
of life while forcing yours upon them in the name of
progress? Will they be considered savages for not believing as
you believe? What isms or ocracies' shall they be ruled
under? How about classism, will they become the poor

proletariat or the bourgeoisie? Before we seek to conquer outer space. We should first work on doing justice for our own earth and the whole human race.

Govern Thy Self

God is your Lord, King and Master, and you are The Governor and Ruler of yourself and those whom you are a guardian over. So please govern with righteousness, equality and justice lest you find yourself governed and ruled by someone else who is evil, unjust and unfit to reign over you.

Police your desires, for if left unchecked they are the criminals and outlaws that will disturb the peace of your city and those whom you have been set to govern over. Manage the economics of your town and find a balance between not spending to much and not greedily with holding what you Lord has given you. Remember that a city or nation in debt is at risk of being enslaved and corrupted with wickedness, and we are slaves of non but The Highest.

Fortify your forts, ensure your soldiers are well trained and prepared for the inevitable fight against those who wish you to fall from grace. Stand your post always being aware of the enemies from without but even more the worst of enemies which are the enemies within.

Discipline is a great friend of a warrior but remember to be flexible and merciful for the strong winds breaks the stiff tree. A healthy and well- educated population is a powerful population, so ensure that your pantries are filled with good nutritious food and remember waste not, want not!

Make your libraries as vast as those of old Alexandria, allowing all your citizens to be scholars at heart. Evolve and progress, but never trample on others as your society moves forward for the entire universe is justly balanced so if you interrupt that balance in any way, justice will always be reestablished but not in your favor.

Ban fornication, adultery, homosexuality and all other sexual perversions. Reflect on human history and you will find the stories of nations and towns that have fallen because of these deeds. The bond between man and woman is sacred, being a grand union established by the Highest, so do not interrupt it nor attempt to change the nature of it.

Humble yourselves and do away with foolish pride. No matter what heights you reach do not take yourselves for deities or you will become as other nations who have gone before you.

Govern Thy Self

The City

The sounds of the city aren't always pretty,

Air pollution from the cars and industrial areas make the air quality shitty. Today I read about the increasing violence in the paper,

And there's not enough money to raise the teacher's wages, and fund education yet it seems there is plenty of money to fund wars, help other countries and build luxury skyscrapers.

The smell of legalized marijuana fills the air as the consistent flow of alcohol temporarily washes away the people's worries and cares.

Blue collar or white collar, they're always focused on survival,

A pack of beer, bottle of whisky and a pack of cigarettes is his evening revival.

He holds on tight to his last few strings of hope,

But I guess he's better off than the man on the corner finding pleasure in a needle filled with dope.

But here in this place everyone has their drug of choice to cope. The innocent children become casualties of violence,

The victims of rape and molestation fears nobody will hear their story so some of them suffer in silence.

I can feel the city ebb and flow,

And what will happen in the next few moments, only God truly knows.

The ambulance's sirens echo in the distance and I can only wonder who has died,

I guess whoever they are they are finally free from this city and will cross over the great divide.

Little boy child, who are you going to grow up to be?

Right now, you're just a mirror reflecting everything you see.

Little girl I fear that soon there will be no innocence left in your eyes

And you've been hurt so much by men that it is them that you despise, She often wishes that she could fly,

But in the darkness of the night, she cuts at her wrist hoping that she would die.

The sounds of the city aren't always pretty.

The Wise Man

An old wise man sat meditating as another man approached him looking as if he had journeyed from a far place. All the signs of one who has been through extreme hardship was upon him from his disheveled hair to the shoes that split opened revealing his feet that were darkened from the dirt of the ground.

He sat in front of the old wise man trying hard to catch his breath, then he said, "Excuse me, I come to you seeking knowledge about things that I do not yet know. My life has been difficult and many mistakes I have made over the years. I've read book after book in search of the answers, many of men whom I thought were wise I've sought counsel with hoping that they could offer me understanding yet they have spoken nothing but fancy words and have given me no solutions. I even asked the stars and constellations for directions, but they rise and set, and I find myself more lost than I already was.

A Sufi told me of you and stated that I would have to travel far to speak to you but the knowledge I would gain would make every step worth it so here I am Old Wise one, tell me the keys to my success." The wise man remained still, eyes closed and seeming to continue with his meditation unbothered by this person who sat before him.

The traveler jumped to his feet angrily, breathing heavily and stated,

"these feet of mine pain me from such a long journey. My back bent from

carrying a load that has become unbearable. Open your eyes and look at me and you will see the bags under my eyes, for sleep teases me for a moment then abandons me.

Many mountains I have climbed and the blisters upon my hands prove that fact. I come not as a beggar, if your advice comes at a cost, I am more than willing to pay it so please name your price. I sacrificed my food and even water to taste of your wisdom, have a sip of your knowledge and to rest upon the pillows of your understanding.

Please do not remain silent, end your long meditation and answer my appeals for help! The path has been difficult for me, yet here I stand before you seeking guidance. Many pleasures of the world I have relinquished, my children left behind and desires unfulfilled in a quest that has brought me here, have you no words for me?"

The Wise man remained silent continuing his meditation as the visitor threw up his hands screaming, "ah old man you know nothing, and you have wasted my time!" As the traveler angrily walked away the wise man said, "if you are always this quick to anger and are impatient, all that you strive so hard for will easily be lost, your struggles to find what you seek will be wasted and you will spend the rest of your life pursuing but gaining nothing, then you will spend the last of you years bitter and filled with regret. When you control your emotions and learn true patience you will find that you already have all that you desire."

The Visitor

Death came to visit today, taking a soul whose appointed time had come.

The sounds of sirens filled the morning air just as the sun was rising from its place in the east.

One man tripped as he climbed up the stairs seeming nervous and knowing that death already came and went.

As I glanced out my window, watching the goings on of this new morning, I took it all as a sign meant for my eyes to see reminding me that death is always near.

Zipped up in the body bag the remains of the person was carefully carried down to be taken away and prepared for its next place of rest.

Today death came to visit, and the faces of this person's beloved were filled with tears, seeming unable to comprehend that this person whom they spoke with yesterday they will never speak to again at least in this realm of existence.

Today I awoke and went about my day, but today someone took their last breath.

June 1, 2019

THE EXTRACTION

Shall we carry this soul to the depths of hell or to the gardens of paradise? Many are its deeds, some good and some are bad, but the creation fulfilled its appointed time on the earth, now We have been commanded to take away that which none, but the One can give back.

Oh Lord how do You wish for Us to extract this soul? Your Will shall be done, and We are ones to carry out Your orders with not an atoms weight of rebellion or doubt. Our fellow brethren have witnessed and recorded his deeds, but even with all our scribes and watchers surely You are All Knowing.

If good our extraction shall be swift and painless, but if evil we shall tear at him violently and he will grasp at this life begging for another chance but his pleads will go unheard and he shall know of no peace in any part of this process. Those who cursed him life might rejoice for his departing while those who loved him will shed tears today. Praise be to You Most High, The One who creates life and can take it away, We are Your servants here to fulfill a duty, so how shall We extract this soul?

The Message

Oh, young soul, I'll tell you a thing of great importance, In hopes that you will take heed to the things I say.

Do Not Waste Time

For time is beyond precious and I would advise you to make use of it now while you are young, and your strength is still with you.

To squander time is a crime against yourself and you deny others the beauty of your talents.

Do not allow yourself to grow old, bitter and filled with regret, lying on the bed of misery, telling the same sad stories of, "should have, could have, would have," burning in the emotional flames because, "you didn't."

Oh, how the hourglass has turned, with the sands of time in your youth swiftly emptying out into old age until there is not a single grain left.

Discover the greatness within yourself, cherish every moment, respect time and you will find that time is more than willing to work to your benefit.

Do Not Waste Time!

The Humans

What is this strange creation called human? Over time they have populated the earth by the billions. They are as the flowers in a great garden for they come in a variety of shades and types each unique yet on the basic biological level they all seem the same.

Are they some form of higher animal? Doesn't the other mammal species have two eyes to see, two ears to hear and one mouth with which to consume and communicate? I will not get into details about their profound desire to mate which has allowed them to supposedly start from two to many and some have little to no shame in their intimate dealings, in fact the lower animals seem more modest than them at times. The animals of the earth are made up of different communities and so it seems the same with the humans and diverse are their languages, spiritual beliefs and even their styles of expressing themselves via their art forms are amazing. Such a young creation that has come so far and within their history is so much tragedy and death, yet we still wonder what is this human thing and why does it exist? Walking upright upon the lands and using their hands as a tool to handle and manipulate the world around them. The birds, bees, ants, etc., build their homes and communities going about daily existence and the humans do the same also. From small villages to huge metropolises, they build with desires of reaching to the heavens and the mysteries of some of their past brethren they have yet to even solve, but their desire for knowledge has always been strong though they attempt to withhold some information and hide it which this form of deception has and will continue to hold them back.

Every creature has an enemy it must fight against and protect their communities from, yet it seems humanity is its own worst enemy, fighting over their differences, the same differences that make them unique and beautiful. Then there is their strange pursuit for material possessions that drives them to greed, war and the destruction of their only home and possibly even their own existence.

The stronger amongst them rule the weaker with the intentions of gaining more wealth and power. At points of human history, the weak have been forced in servitude, building the great thrones and empires of their overlords. What strange power these rulers must have to be in control of so many while they are so few, but through our observations we have seen the turning of the tide as those few under the leadership of one did rise for freedom.

Moving forward, much has changed in the passage of time, yet still even in their more subtle forms things remains the same and much progress is needed for the development of humans. Through all the tragedy, great humans always come forward and do amazing things, changing the course of their worlds, but if only they would come together and realize that they are one.

This human thing is a strange thing indeed!

FAKE NEWS

Fake news is nothing new, it has just become easier to spread
since the advance of technology. Hidden agendas and plans
of men who rewrite history and feed the masses what they
desire them to have, even religion is watered down and the
so-called practitioners of it are evil and paganistic themselves.
The truth is powerful and supposedly has the ability if
properly used to set the people free, but how do you set a
people free if they have been convinced by false information
that they are not slaves?

Destiny

Today I went on a journey yet walked nowhere at all,
Feeling as the earth tilted and the seasons changed from
spring, summer and the browning of the leaves for fall.
The sun rising and setting at the two east and the two west.
Then I found myself setting under a tree where the creatures
of the day found rest and there I rested also.
Today I time traveled to yesterday hoping to gain a deeper
understanding of who I am today, yet the past was already
broken and scattered vanishing into the void transforming
into small pieces of sand and matter, I even attempted to
speak to the people, yet they heard me not.
Today I tried peering into the future, yet I saw nothing,
except a mirrored veil that simply reflected to me the current
image of myself. Frustrated I began to make plans, then
thoughts of all type began to overtake me, and I found myself
becoming anxious, so I stopped, threw my hands up and

decided that I will be Destiny's captured slave allowing her to drag me
where she will, and I can only hope that she we be kind.

ORDO

I've heard many speak about the coming of a time where there will be one currency for the entire world and no borders shall exist with the planet being under the rule of a single government, but will the masses of this world willingly accept this or must chaos first be introduced until the people gladly take whatever form of order is given to them?

Catastrophic collisions from that which falls from the heavens, decimation of a large percentage of the world population via drought, famine, pandemics and or record-breaking natural disasters, what will be the turning point that will make all nations declare a state of international emergency?

The great protocol has begun, and world governments have prepared for the fall. Behold the wrath of heavens furry, oceans spilling over, and the earth shaking. Desperation has driven the people mad as they run about looking for food and water and their despair drives some of them to rage and violence. The senate is silent and even the military has indulged in the ongoing ferocity. The grid is down, and lack of technology and communications networks has brought all planes to the ground.

Preachers on the street corners are yelling, "Jesus is the only way, so come to The Lord and seek forgiveness for your sins before Judgement Day," the Muslims are in the mosque performing Salat as the Imam reminds the Ummah that the fires of hell hot, yet there is mercy for the true believer and the Rabbi has the full attention of the entire Synagogue while speaking in Hebrew the Word of God. The sun has set many of hours ago, yet fires light up the cities and at this this time man is truly lost.

World leaders have gathered secretly to figure out how to bring about order, with plans to lock down the cities and establish organization at all borders. "The need for control is obvious, so contact central command and inform them that we must have the full cooperation of all leaders to establish a new course for the world." Martial law is now established, the military has brought order to the streets and buildings that were once grocery stores have been changed to government-controlled detention centers. All light rail and public transport have been seized to carry the people to camps all over the cities and the sound of a mother crying can be heard as she is separated from her children, unsure if she will ever see them again.

Camp wards are set up with Ward One being for men, Ward Two for children 7 and up, and Ward Three for women and children 6 and below. The men are put to labor to build and those who refuse are severely punished. All buildings that were once detention centers are soon

renamed, "Assessment and Reprogramming Facilities."

Punishment is now a community event witnessed by all in hopes to curve thoughts of dissidence, and with the new grid up and running, all are chipped and numbered. Unmanned aircraft hover around the new Smart Cities scanning for rebels and their children who try to remove themselves from the newly established order.

Governments have created, "New World Eugenics Centers," and individuals must have permission to mate and reproduce, but those who refuse, their children are forcibly aborted and both sterilized and separated.

The Beginning of The New World Order is Established.

BLACK

Perhaps they figure since they listen to the music, dress and act out the so-called "Swagger" they are black. They'll even switch lingo I guess believing that speaking Ebonics makes them relatable and therefore easier to approach one whom they consider black. It's laughable when they quote rap lyrics from rap songs while looking at another black person for approval as if saying, "I'm down with your culture can't you see. If one doesn't follow the created stereotype than are they not being black, because their version of black doesn't match what's portrayed in music and T.V.? What is black and how does one who is black act? Shall he sing and dance for you to make you feel better, shall he tell you jokes and be your dark jester, or is dark skin part of a secret twisted sexual fantasy? What did you learn about black people in school or better yet in the living rooms of your family members? Was it the limited information about slavery, Emancipation Proclamation and Martin Luther King's "Dream?"This message is to my own not just to other non-black people, because we are guilty of furthering our own oppression and self-hate. Parading in the streets screaming, "Black Lives Matter," yet in our neighborhoods the murder of each other we propagate. For a check from the movie and music companies we gladly push the agenda, professing brotherhood to all mankind. Yet amongst each other we hardly find a piece of mind. Then there are those who love to revel in the greatness of ancient African past, but what are we doing to bring forward black greatness in the future?

Time and Youth

Let us look beyond the follies of our youth as they pass, and we enter the midpoint of this journey. All that I truly will miss is the boldness, oh how bold and daring the young are, willing to take chances worrying about risk later, unwilling to conform to the ways set by those who are old and rigid, and the beauty of their rebellion is despised by the conformist, but all praise be to the new innovators.

For now, this hair turns white with time and Lord Willing patience becomes a part of my once fiery character. Oh, how I am looking forward to an increase in wisdom, a continued quest for knowledge that never ends and seeking first to understand and then be understood to grasp a clear view on human nature. Mirrors and hour glasses remind us of our mortality, but narcissist must pull away from his reflection and take account of the world around him before he perishes knowing nothing except the beauty of his past that has gone away, trapped in his own visual deception while the world and those who desire him calls out his name hoping to indulge in the pleasure of his presence but he is so full of himself that he denies others his time and is cursed for doing so.

The elder stares at the youth as they pass by and such splendor it is as the elder man remembers when he was handsome and strong, and the elder woman smile as she sees the youth filled lady whose skin is tight yet soft and gravity has yet to pull down the things that are part of the feminine adornments. They are swift and move as the wind while believing their days of being young are forever.

Elder eyes envelope great libraries of knowledge and wisdom that they wish to pass on before their journey, for what good will it do in the grave. Few of the youth stop for a moment and listen, yet one day they will when the barriers of time slow down their steps. Their brilliant rebellions make them the innovators for tomorrow, fighters of what seems new wars many of which are problems from the past started by those before them but to them the world is new, and they would believe they have the solutions to solve all the problems and perhaps they do but sometimes the elders are not willing to lend an ear to someone they feel has no experience and time. The youth seek guidance, but they are not interested in old foolishness that brings no solutions and the world continues to push back but so do they, so they fight and rebel until the goings on in the world begins to consume them with being busy and they begin to age and watch new youths be born and the cycle repeats itself repeatedly.

From the womb we come forth, going through the beautiful blossoming springs and summers of our lives. At a point fall comes and wrinkles the leaves we call flesh, and the inevitable cold death of winter brings all to an end.

New Exodus

Surely it must be time for the tables to be turned, and the Pharaohs have ruled for too long. They have burdened the people long with their cruelty, taxed us beyond what we can stand, and sent our sons and daughters off to fight their senseless wars. We have worked hard only to give our earnings right back to them and become their indebted prisoners charged high interest rates with no relief in sight. Their bellies are full, and they feast even more while we starve, mocking us as they build lavish places to live and entertain their greedy guest while the hard pavements and underpasses are the places where we dwell.

Their thirst is quenched from clean waters, while we are sickened from the polluted waters that even the animals refuse to drink from. They pass us in their grand chariots looking down as if they are gods and we are worthless beings to be trampled over and when they commit crimes against us justice seems to turn a blind eye, yet if we even speak ill of them, we are stripped of what little we have.

We are free to elect whosever they select from among themselves, so no matter what, their agendas get fulfilled while nothing changes here. Their guards beat and abuse us patrolling our neighborhoods, but they don't seem to realize they are slaves to the pharaohs who should be working with us instead of against us and we are educated not to be intelligent but to be obedient patriotic servants to king and country though king and country does not serve us.

Shall the waters be turned to blood, skies plagued with locust, and will death visit the sons of our tyrannical rulers? We are a people held in awe of the magic shown to us, but we are beginning to see past their trickery and deception. Guide us oh Moses from this place and split the seas that we may pass, but surely some of us are a rebellious people choosing the ways of their former masters though you have shown us better. Warning after warning the Pharaohs have been sent, but they are arrogant and prideful, so death and destruction of them and their nation is the only solution.

Guide us through this new Exodus to The Promised Land.

The Path

An old wise man sat dying, so he prepared himself for the moving forward, praying, meditating and putting his things in order to make the parting easy for his family but a thought of great importance shook him, so he called upon those who scribe his words for he had been unable to write as his hands were unsteady being nervous about his meeting in the afterlife.

"My scribes, write down all that I say, and I shall keep it simple, but fill your writing tools that they may not run dry and interrupt my words. The paper you press these upon must be strong enough to pass through the hardships of time so that future generations may read them and take heed to what is said. The instructions are simple so tell them:

Do not be led astray by the foolishness that surrounds you, in fact learn to choose your companions in this life well for they will be of great influence on you and you on them. The path to greatness may at times seem a long and harsh road but be patient and do not rush into situations that slow or completely stop your progress. If you are young, immediately

seek to control that which is between your legs and your two jaw bones for they are the things that can easily destroy all that you strive to build.

No matter what you are told nor how many people you see indulging in it, do not let the strong drink touch your lips for it corrupts and destroys so it is a thing I advise you to stay far away from no matter how tempted you may become. Deal with the hardships of life better yet embrace them, with patience and endurance they will strengthen you, but if you choose to sedate yourself as the others do you may stunt your own growth and development.

Cherish your mind, it has been created by One Who created all things, so please stay far away from substances that alter it. In some of the leaves and herbs of the earth there are great medical benefits but don't be as the fools who have come to abuse them using them for sport and play, changing what has been perfected, all that you need you already have and through practice you can activate what is within you without the use of chemical influence which over time weakens many of your powerful abilities, and lastly control your emotions especially anger, for in a fit a rage a person can say and or do things that will make you lose in seconds what may have taken you years to build."

The old wise looked upon his scribes smiling content with what he had left.

BEYOND THIS INFERNO

Just as Dante,' at the midpoint journey of my life, I realized that I messed up and the straight path was lost. Finding myself wondering in these concrete jungles, I began to witness some of the levels of this hell and its tenants. Sad were the faces in these dark places, unable to escape the trials and tribulations their own deeds had brought upon them. The ghetto pits burned with the rages of men and fiery lust of women.

Such a pity to see torn and burned flesh from the gun fire piercing in and exploding outwards, I began to ask of what dark form of art is this?

Confused I was at the level where the suicides dwell, so I asked, "oh child why have you hanged yourself, so pure and innocent so what has brought you to this horrible end of self-mutilation?" In response she said, "The cold words of the other children in life have broken me along with the chaos of my own home so I no longer saw reason to live." Tears fell from her eyes as the sound of children taunting and laughing with devilish voices echoed in this fiery pit.

"Oh, woman what has come of you, you are covered with filthy, diseased, and puss filled wounds, yet you dare to tempt me? "Vengeance!" she screamed. "My lust caught up with me and men filled me with disease so I sought to make others suffer and feel my pain, what is wrong mortal man, do you not lust for me also surely that must be the sin that has brought you to this dark alley way where the fires of lust burn? Between her legs rested serpents with fangs trapping and paralyzing all who laid with her, and many were the burning souls who rested beside her engulfed in the flames of passion.

The pit got hotter as I approached a huge building on fire which held a broken cross upon it. I realized it was a church but written on the walls were words, "House of Hypocrites and Liars." The preacher stood at the pulpit with a gun to his head and said before pulling the trigger, "The Lord will not forgive me for these sins and abominations I have committed." The congregation turned and looked at me as the flames engulfed them all

screaming, "we knew yet said nothing."

As I walked deeper into this place of black smoke and tormented souls, I bumped into a drunkard whose eyes were sunken in and dark and in his hand was a bottle filled with boiling puss and as he tilted it back to drink, it burned and melted his face with the strange liquid oozing from the many parts of his body. He stumbled away yelling, "it's killing me, but I just can't stop!" The smell of rotting flesh filled the air and a man with the words "junky" cut into his face held a serpent with exposed fangs and he violently shoved the fangs into his arms and many more serpents were consuming his feet and biting at his neck and the serpents hissed, "we are his masters, and he is our slave."

Woe this dark place! The levels of treachery and betrayal and even worse was the blood soaked pavement where brothers and family ripped at each other's flesh, some draped in blue others in red, hurled wicked epithets at each other while gnawing away at the faces of those whom they were supposed to love, but anger consumed them as they dragged each other away into the fiery caskets bound by boiling and sticky blood, surrounded by a burning wall where there names where written with the hot coals of hell.

I found no Virgil to guide me through this place and I feared my deeds in life had brought me here for I was neither dead nor living, and contrary to beliefs I found no devil ruling here, no Prince of Darkness only humanity consumed by their vile ways. Burdened by all that I witnessed I fell to my knees for all hope I had abandoned, and my religion was lost and there seemed to be nothing left Beyond this Inferno.

Journey Between Two Worlds

From the time of our conception until our final breath we are on a journey and according to what I have read in all religions and the different spiritual beliefs man holds dear, even the thing we know as death is not the end of our journey, but who has come back to tell? Surely, I know not for I can only quote what I have read and learned from others many of whom opinions and ideas of life and death have become popular among the human family, but I find it hard to believe that a being of superior intelligence would waste anything even a human soul, if that is what it is called and with all things held up with true balance and justice will a person live a life of good or evil and not be properly judged for their deeds? In due time we all will learn the truth of that matter.

That light at the end of the tunnel, perhaps it is the first rays of the outside world observed through the blurry vision of new eyes coming forth from the womb after a long journey from the tomb and through the halls of some sort of afterlife and a reincarnation or rebirth of sort. Such a joy it is for all to see welcoming this new person into this existence, pure and untainted by the world and all its ways, blank is the mind except what may have been heard in the womb.

Hands touch what has not yet been touched and the sound of this new world becomes somewhat overbearing, but the love of the mother and the nurturing food from her calms all internal confusion. The physical connections are cut but bonds reconnect what may never be severed. Helpless we are for a period of time, yet it all comes full circle for if we live long enough we may grow old and return to that state of helplessness in need of assistance from another loving human being, but let us deal with the phase of youthfulness for at this time we are a person trying to find ourselves, understand the world and find what our place is in it, mimicking that which we see and hear from those who have been here longer thinking that perhaps they have the answers to that which we seek, but we seek to find our own personality and own ways sometimes assuming that our adventure is of something new and different and the difficulties faced can be solved with solutions that we think are something unlike all the rest of those around us and the elders laugh and shake their heads as we fall and stumble upon paths that many have already walked, but they must learn on their own, journeying along the path way of experience and one day they will be the wise elders watching a new generation do the same. Until then, theirs is a beautiful rebellion with dreams of changing the world with their visions of the future seen through naïve but beautiful and pure eyes.

A pleasure it is to see young love, two youths experiencing the bonds that can be felt between human beings as they glance into each other's eyes, holding hands with intentions of taking on the cold world together preferring to die before ever being taken apart. Romantic tales and plays all through human history imitate this part of the human experience, but tragic is the heartache when a young heart is broken for the first time, it is as if their whole world has come crumbling apart and they hide in the darkness hoping no one will see the tears they shed and as far as they are concerned no one can comprehend what they are going through as if it is a thing never experienced before by any, yet soon enough they learn it is a thing that is part of the journey of life.

Loss tends to be another cruel companion who catches up with us at certain points of our lives, coming in its many different forms, such as loss of friends, family, love, health, wealth and some people even lose their minds, but let us not forget the many joys that come, because to focus only on the negative is truly a waste of precious time. I prefer the beauty and contagiousness of a smile and those moments of pleasure that makes being a human such a wonderful thing, enjoyable to see and hear like the giggle of a child rolling around uncontrollably smiling and loving even the simplest things in life, perhaps if we were to be as them this world would be an amazing place.

The whole world rides on the waves of musical notes, with the power of sound causing the people to get up and dance, with a tune that causes two to make love while lost in the erotic melodies. The drums bring a whole village into a trance stomping foot upon the earth, electric vibes pulsating through the air, as the keys make bodies shake screaming out testimonies of experiencing holy spirits. A child is born an elder die but perhaps all this is just a journey between two worlds.

The Temptress

I lust for her in ways that I shouldn't. Burning inside with desire, imagination running wild but what good is all this imagination if it cannot be brought into reality. Dabbling in fantasy, aroused by fictional actions that I'm sure would be more pleasurable in the realm of true human contact. Yet the signs are all clear from my own experience that nothing good will come out of these deeds of fornication, laying on a bed engulfed in the flames, flesh burning all in the pursuit of a moment of pleasure, tilting the scales and changing the turning of Fortuna's Wheel, to that of loss and despair.

Yet she tempts me with a stare that hardens my nature, and I would surely fill her womb with new life if only it was not so wrong. Who will judge and stone this wicked adulterous affair, cutting the hands of the thief who steals her away when her husband goes to tend to his business, yet this is just my mind running wild wishing to fill and touch her lips while

also knowing what will be the consequence of such deeds which will bring about unwanted problems and the satisfaction for a day of pleasure is not worth the long term loss of blessings that will come after it, so for now I will silence these desires and reframe from the intentions in my head.

Who am I fooling? I have always been one to play along the thin lines of temptation, so close to the waters edge and many times I have fallen in almost drowning if not for the guidance of One who has pulled me from the waters when I have gone astray, but the dog has returned to his vomit just as the fool has returned to his folly and I always find my self laying beside the temptress naked yet covered in shame, no fig leaves to hide my deeds from The One that sees all.

At times I subtly seduce her in hopes she makes a move on me so I may pretend she is the one seducing and I am the innocent soul trying to escape her advances, that I may place the blame on her if caught by her lover. Vile are these ways of the slithering snake who uses deception to trap his pray only to find himself crushed under the feet of universal justice and the husband is right in his violent dealings with the deceptive snake as Adam should have done in the Garden.

I know well the ending of this endeavor, but the blood and my mind has found its way to my other head and short sighted is that which sees only with one eye and I have heard the call of my Lord, the signs are clear, and the warnings announced, but my lower desires have not ears with which to hear, it wishes only to be enveloped in the womb of the temptress and straight is this path to hell that leads to her bedroom where I am to rest.

KINGDOMS

They rise, They fall,

They come and they go,

Some last for short periods of time, while others endure and how they will end nobody, but God truly knows. Starts as an idea in the minds of men,

A land full of potential is where it all begins, The rivers flow and the grains are good,

Religious centers for their deities rise from brick and wood. The citizens look upon the men whom they see as just and fair,

The walls of capitols are built in hopes the seats of law and order will be established there.

Gather the master builders to establish the corner stone, Under these celestial bodies millions will call this home. Command the farmers to prepare the land,

So, there is bread and meat for every child, woman and man. Let not the youth run amuck,

Some will become educated scholars; some manual workers and we will take soldiers from those strong young bucks.

Disciplined men and women will watch over this place,

Declaring war on any outsider who dares to smite a single citizens face. Welcome the traveler and give him a place to rest,

Let them dine and feast among us if evil intent is not hidden within his chest.

If the scales of justice are balanced, no worries there will be,

The ground will bear fruits and vegetables and fish shall be our blessing from the sea,

Woe that day when the scales tilt away from what is moral and good, Our nation will be as the fool lost in a dark wood,

Stumbling and never finding a grip,

Our leaders will become corrupted, setting us in troubled waters and selfishly abandoning the ship.

The internal structures of the family will begin to fall apart,

And from that point the fall of our once mighty nation will start.

The seeds of men will release their frustration and rage through violence, Our places of worship will become empty and silent.

Blind eventually justice will be,

Unable to stop the greedy from destroying our land and seas. The truth will become despised,

With the people being content with lies. Judges for a price will set the criminal free,

Out of fear people will turn their heads away from the wickedness they know they see.

Sad will be the day when the good are mocked and scorned, While the wicked is held up high and adored.

Strong opiate and drink will become the new solution,

And if the people are entertained, they will step over their dying brothers and pretend they are ok with the pollution.

Man and woman will know no shame,

They will give away all honor and dignity for a short

moment of fame,

Yet die full of regret,

Children so lost and depressed that they slice at their own wrist and necks. Foreign invaders will sense the decay from far away,

And the once mighty nation will be conquered and slayed. Kingdoms rise and kingdoms fall.

Power of the Pen

My pen wishes to speak, and it refuses to remain silent,
calling upon me in the night and the early parts of the
morning, commanding me to pick it up and write. Who dares
to own a pen and not make use of it for the pen is the greatest
companion of the one who thinks and when the mind is filled
and prepared to spill over the pen is the key that unlocks
those gates so that the thoughts may freely flow?

What is a swords man who does not practice using his
sword? Every day he puts time into his craft sharpening his
skills and the sword itself and he is not one to set the sword
down for long periods of time allowing himself and the
sword to become dull, please know and understand that the
pen is my sword.

The scattered brain is organized by the pen, commanding
this army of thoughts to stand in formation by ranks, each
soldier in its position prepared for the war of words.
Speaking of war, many treatises in history bled with ink to
keep from spilling the blood of men, praise be the
peacekeeper who wields the power of the pen so there is no
need to wield the sword.

Oh woman, shall I caress thee and hold you in my arms

melting your heart away with each stroke. You have submitted your body to me but before this encounter it was the pen and the words which flowed and enticed your soul, giving me full access to your mind, fingering the hidden places that only writers and men skilled in music can touch, your orgasm is beyond the superficial levels that you've become use to, she is a slave to the pen that seduces and drives to the point of obsession.

The pen has brought about the greats such as William Shakespeare, Charles Dickens, Mark Twain, Edgar Allan Poe, and those are just a few of those who enticed the world with the power of the pen. Etched are their names, permanently written in the ever-flowing waves of time, to be rehearsed, rewritten, respoken, but let the pens with which they wrote with be sealed away forever never to be touched again by men.

Oh, how the most important parts of history would be lost if not for those who scribe and embrace the pen, though many in time erase the truth, rewriting words to fit their own opinions and agendas, somewhere the truth is hidden in a cave revealing what the liars wished would never be discovered, and when the walls are torn down, light shined into the dried empty ancient wells, when the stones have been pulled back and the tombs and it scrolls have been discovered, and when nature and the secrets of her words are seen written deep in the scrolls of the unseen heavens, when the waters are pulled back, and ink tattooed skin of an old king is found we will know what has been forgotten.

Do not deny the pen when it calls upon you to write for even in the time of war and loneliness it can be your best of friend. Oh, prison guards give your prisoners pens with which to write so they may free themselves and not be consumed by their own thoughts which can drive some to the point of madness, for the pen may not remove the physical bars and concrete but it will take them places beyond a cell and help them to discover the answers that may one day free them from mental and maybe even physical bondage.

The pen and the gift of writing is truly a powerful gift from The Highest, Lord bless the pen.

LOSER

Some would speak highly of me as if I was one to never do wrong, but for me to say that it would all be a lie,

there are no halos on this head so during my funeral let them not speak sweet falsehood after I die.

Let not my critics remain silent,

In fact, I'll say it for them, I spent most of my youth in juvenile hall, then at 18 I entered prison for a crime of violence.

That old lady didn't deserve the pain that we caused,

I'm sure she didn't awaken that day expecting to get robbed. So, call me a thug, convict, criminal, whatever you wish to say,

Just keep my father's name out your mouth, for it was I who chose to go astray.

As a single hard-working father, he did the best that he could,

Raised me in South Central L.A. trying hard to shelter me from the madness of the hood.

The prodigal son I became,

He knew when I left for Denver, Colorado I would never be the same. Yes, I've been a loser,

Hardened heart, angry at the world and perhaps I was a woman abuser,

Ask Andrea, Porsche' and Melicya and hear some of the stories they must tell,

But it is my children who suffer with this hell.

I am that absent father who shows up every once and a while, But the innocence of a child still allows them to smile. I know the day will come when they will be older,

I fear that they will look at old me and give me the cold shoulder. All those who loved me ever wanted was a little bit of my time, But I chose to remain isolated stuck in my own mind.

I'm guilty of being a hypocrite,

And all the reading I do, and righteousness I talk doesn't mean shit. On the outside I seem so happy and sure, But inside my heart is dark, and I am hateful and insecure. Sad is the life of the loser.

The Prisoner

Prison? Yea I've been there too 108855,

I'm aware of the mental and emotional damage that solitary confinement can do.

When the phone calls go unanswered and the letters stop coming, all you look forward to is that day when you are free so you can hit the ground running,

but until than it is just marked off places on the calendar and the shorter the time,

the more the thoughts about freedom plays on your mind.

Every day is just another day,

An empty void to be filled so of course some get religion to find their way, Heavy are the burdens of sins,

Setting down that load only happens when the gates are closed so behind those walls is where the real journey for finding oneself begins.

Feeling like an animal caged,

An explosive concoction of too much testosterone (for the women locked up, estrogen) and rage,

I can hear the steel being sharpened in the night,

Pushups and weight training are mandatory just in case of a fight. Never been a victim of sodomy, but the victim's eyes tell no lies, Some will never see freedom or feel the softness of a woman's thighs, And their manhood is shook,

Some wisely invest their time improving themselves with advanced education and books.

The self-educated seem to set themselves free realizing, "You can imprison my body, but my mind belongs to me." Dark is that twenty-three and one,

The moment when the body is still yet the mind begins to run. Bouncing back and forth off the walls,

Walking so close to the edge until you mentally take that fall. Deep into that abyss,

You feel the poisonous touch of insanities kiss.

It's no more than your subconscious mind revealing the truth about who you are,

And behind that brick and steel you can't run far.

Back to population, black and Mexicans on one side, whites on the other,

A world divided by internal gang politics and color.

The broken and lost souls of society are your neighbors,

Clothes, furniture, even licenses plates are the products of the new slave labor.

The good amongst the prison guard are few,

But give any person a little power over another human being and watch what they will do.

To those on the outside world, if you can't do the time than don't do the crime,

But to you brothers and sisters in prison look deep within and that piece of mind you will find.

When you finally do get free . . . NEVER LOOK BACK NEVER LOOK BACK NEVER LOOK BACK!!!!

God bless the prisoners.

Acknowledgments

This book is dedicated to my father who has been and still is a great motivator and inspiration, to my mother who no matter how difficult things have been has always stood beside me, even through my times of trouble and rebellion. To my big brother Mike who has been a guide through the difficulties and has always strived to be the bond to keep family connected. To my sons Jibreel and Dante' Jr. thank you for your patience, good times are coming. Nancy Viera, if it wasn't for you these writings would just be words written in notebooks unshared. Thank you so much for your help and being my enlightenment me through this new journey and hopefully the many more to come.

I was born July 2, 1982 to Floyd P. Duruisseau and Sheila Robinson in Denver, Colorado. After my mother and father separated, my dad took on the task of raising me. We moved to Los Angeles, California in 1988 and from that point until 1998, I experienced the world of Compton and South Central Los Angeles. My father was born and raised in Compton (Willowbrook), so that world (including riots) was nothing new to him, but it was new to me.

In mid 1998 I returned to Denver, Colorado to live with my mother and 1999 was the beginning year for my time of rebellion and trouble from juvenile hall until 18 years old and the tuff world of Prison cells. I was a young man trying to find my way and over time I did, which is a blessing or else you probably wouldn't be reading this book now and my journey at forty years old is only just beginning.

Dante Duruisseau

* * *

You can find Dante on Instagram @danteduruisseau